Dedicated to all our beautiful children for a thousand generations.

Baby Blessings
Rebecca Morris

All rights reserved. No part of this publication may be reproduced, distributed, or transmitted in any form or by any means, including photocopying, recording, or other electronic or mechanical methods, without the prior written permission of the publisher.

ISBN: 978-0-6485847-2-8
eBook ISBN: 978-0-6485847-3-5

Published by Seraph Creative in 2019 - seraphcreative.org

www.rebeccamorris.art

Thankyou to Lindi Masters
for all your love and
support

A special Thankyou to
Pete and Fiona Mack

My wonderful husband and
father of our children
David

Beauty of blessings

The Word of God is living and full of power.
When you decree and declare god's word, it promises to bring itself to pass.

The blessings we speak are infused with incredible sovereignty to create life.

'Decree a thing and it will be established' Job 22:28

BLESSING YOUR BABY,
I HAVE COME TO BELIEVE

"IS AN ORIENTATION OF THE **SPIRIT**,
AN ORIENTATION OF THE **HEART**;
IT TRANSCENDS THE WORLD
THAT IS IMMEDIATELY EXPERIENCED, AND IS
ANCHORED SOMEWHERE BEYOND ITS
HORIZONS."

("HOPE,' VACLAV HAVEL, *DISTURBING THE PEACE* [NEW YORK: KNOPF, 1990] P.181)

INTENTIONALLY CULTIVATING A **SACRED SPACE** EACH DAY TO BLESS YOUR BABY, IS LIKE CREATING AND TENDING A BEAUTIFUL GARDEN IN THE SPIRIT. YOU ARE AFFIRMING THE BOND BETWEEN BABY AND YOURSELF. THIS STRENGTHENS THE CONNECTION, THE KNOWING AND THE ONENESS RELATIONALLY. THIS BOOK IS LIKE A **LOVE LETTER**, INFUSED WITH WHOLESOMENESS, GOODNESS AND LOVE FOR THE BABY TO REST IN AND DRAW FROM FOREVER.

Children are our treasures. Speaking life over them in the womb sets them up to shine and become all they are destined to be.

Rebecca's book is a key to speaking blessings over our babies in the womb. Her illustrations are heaven breathed, with declarations that proceed from the Throne of Grace.

I highly recommend this book and encourage you to implement speaking these declarations over your love-gifts.

Psalm 127:3-5 The Passion Translation:
Children are God's love-gift; they are Heaven's generous reward.
Children born to a young couple will one day rise to protect and provide for their parents.
Happy will be the couple who has many of them!
A household full of children will not bring shame on your name but victory when you face your enemies, for your offspring will have influence and honour to prevail on your behalf!

Lindi Masters
Ignite Hubs International

I place my hands onto my tummy

Your secret new abode

Dwelling

Resting

Being

Cherished

Thankyou for coming into our family home.

God has blessed you beyond measure, so I declare and decree...

You are a Tree of Life

I bless you

with

unconditional

love

I bless you to know you always belong in our family.

We honour and
welcome you into
our family.

We will dwell together in grace,
rest and safety.

You are flourishing, thriving and growing deeply in the ways of love.

I bless the
good seed
within you
to flourish, multiply
and yield
beautiful fruits

I bless you with loving friends.

You are adored by
Yahweh,
Yeshua,
Holy Spirit
and
all of Heaven.

I bless you
with

Abundance

You are a portal of God's overflowing, abundant goodness.

I bless you to fully love and accept your beautiful self.

You are

a

Citizen of Heaven

I bless the divine technologies within your body to

Awaken,

Burst forth,

Activate!

You are Divine Health!

As God knits you together
in my womb,
I bless every autosome in your
DNA
with wholeness,
victory and love.

You are a Holy Temple.
I call every cell, organ,
bone, joint and system
of your body
to form perfectly.

I bless your eyes to see Heaven!

Yeshua

Angels

Beings

The Cloud of Witnesses

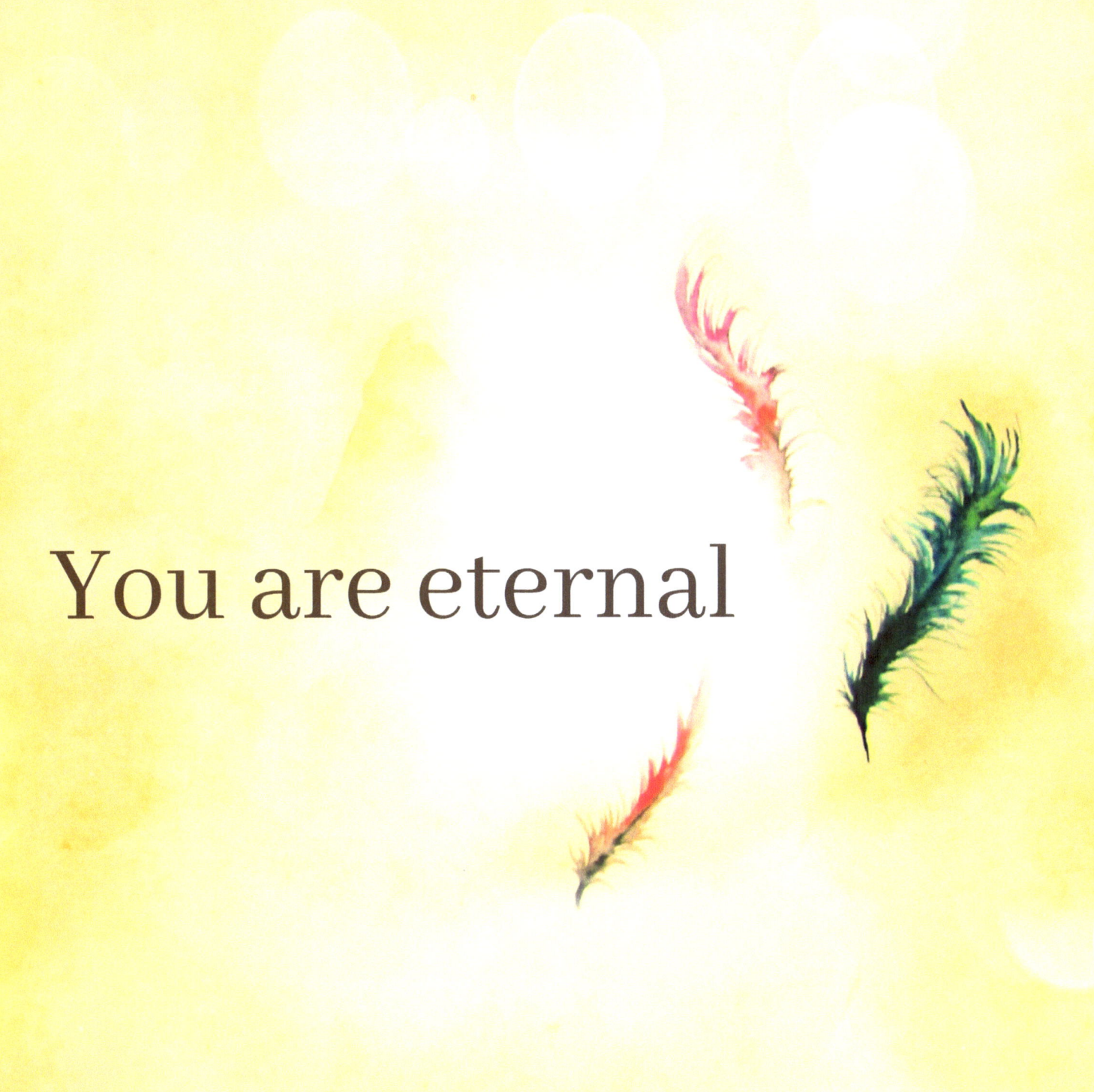

I bless you to build an intimate relationship with God; face to face with Him

YOU ARE THE LIGHT OF THE WORLD

I bless you to shine, glisten and release your light.

You are light.
Kings and nations
will be drawn
to the light of your
shining.

I bless your heart to be completely captivated by Heaven.
I call to rememberance the ancient ways of Yahweh.

You are Ancient

You are a

King

and a Priest .

You are made in God's image!

I bless your tongue to utter mysteries of life.

You are
Holy as He is Holy.

I bless your heart to be set ablaze for the Living word of God.

You are able to use the word of God as a Doorway into Revelation

You are a creator of worlds and galaxies

You are full
of God's love and
power
to bless the
cosmos

You are
an administrator of
Heaven.

I bless you
to know
WISDOM

You are Wise

I bless you to know your future is secure.

I bless your feet to dwell in lush green pastures.

And to run wild and free in fields of grace.

Blessed

with

Righteousness

I bless you
to always know the
Prince of Peace
dwells
within you

I bless you to discover the hidden treasure trove within and to help others discover theirs.

You are joy!

I bless your dreams.

That the
mysteries
would open up
around you
and
engage with you.

You are led by the Holy Spirit.

You are
for
signs and
wonders

You are a worshipper

I bless your scroll.
A beautiful blueprint
of everything
you planned and agreed
to do with God on the
earth for such a time as
this!

You are a beloved son on a great journey into maturity.

Creation waits with eager longing for the revealing of the mature sons of God.

Children are a heritage from the Lord, offspring a reward from Him

Like arrows in the hands of a warrior are children born in one's youth.

Blessed is the man whose quiver is full of them.

the Lord bless you and keep you;
the Lord cause His face
to shine upon you
and be gracious to you;
the Lord turn His face towards you
and give you peace.

Rabbinical Blessing

May you see your world in your lifetime,
May your future be for the life of the world that is coming,
and your hope for generations of generations.

May your heart meditate with understanding,
and your mouth speak wisdoms.
May your tongue be moved to songs.

May your eyelids look straight before you;
May your eyes shine with the light of the Torah,
Your face be radiant, like the brightness of the firmament.

May your lips utter wisdom,
and your kidneys rejoice in righteousness.
May your steps run to hear the words of the Ancient of Days.

www.ingramcontent.com/pod-product-compliance
Lightning Source LLC
Chambersburg PA
CBHW042348300426
44110CB00032B/62